THIS HIKING LOG BOOK
BELONGS TO

_____

_____

_____

HIKING LOGBOOK

Copyright © 2020 by CATIZ PARADI

FIRST EDITION

HIKING

Date

Start Time	
End Time	
Total Duration	
Total Distance	
Elevation Gain/Loss	

Trail Type	Out/Back	Loop	One Way/ Shuttle

Weather   ☐ Cold   ☐ Hot   ☐ Mild

The Hike ☆☆☆☆☆

City / State	
Trail/s	
Start Latitude Longitude	
Terrain	
Cell Phone Reception / Carrier	

☐First Visit ☐Return Visit	Personal Rating	☐ Easy ☐Intermediat ☐Difficult

HIKING

Companion/s	
Facilities / Water Availability	
Trail & Weather Conditions	
Obesrvances	
Gear	
Food & Beverages	

Notes For Next Time

Notes / Journaling

HIKING

Date

Start Time	
End Time	
Total Duration	
Total Distance	
Elevation Gain/Loss	

Trail Type	Out/Back	Loop	One Way/ Shuttle

Weather ☐ Cold ☐ Hot ☐ Mild

The Hike ☆☆☆☆☆

City / State	
Trail/s	
Start Latitude Longitude	
Terrain	
Cell Phone Reception / Carrier	

☐First Visit ☐Return Visit | **Personal Rating** | ☐ Easy ☐Intermediat ☐Difficult

Companion/s	
Facilities / Water Availability	
Trail & Weather Conditions	
Obesrvances	
Gear	
Food & Beverages	

Notes For Next Time

Notes / Journaling

HIKING

Date

Start Time	
End Time	
Total Duration	
Total Distance	
Elevation Gain/Loss	

Trail Type	Out/Back	Loop	One Way/ Shuttle

Weather   ☐ Cold   ☐ Hot   ☐ Mild

The Hike   ☆☆☆☆☆

City / State	
Trail/s	
Start Latitude Longitude	
Terrain	
Cell Phone Reception / Carrier	

☐First Visit ☐Return Visit | **Personal Rating** ☐ Easy ☐Intermediat☐Difficult

Companion/s	
Facilities / Water Availability	
Trail & Weather Conditions	
Obesrvances	
Gear	
Food & Beverages	

Notes For Next Time

Notes / Journaling

HIKING

Date	

Start Time	
End Time	
Total Duration	
Total Distance	
Elevation Gain/Loss	

Trail Type	Out/Back	Loop	One Way/ Shuttle

Weather ☐ Cold ☐ Hot ☐ Mild

The Hike ☆☆☆☆☆

City / State	
Trail/s	
Start Latitude Longitude	
Terrain	
Cell Phone Reception / Carrier	

☐First Visit ☐Return Visit | **Personal Rating** | ☐ Easy ☐Intermediat ☐Difficult

Companion/s	
Facilities / Water Availability	
Trail & Weather Conditions	
Obesrvances	
Gear	
Food & Beverages	

Notes For Next Time

Notes / Journaling

HIKING

	Date

Start Time	
End Time	
Total Duration	
Total Distance	
Elevation Gain/Loss	

Trail Type	Out/Back	Loop	One Way/ Shuttle

Weather	☐ Cold ☐ Hot ☐ Mild

The Hike ☆☆☆☆☆

City / State	
Trail/s	
Start Latitude Longitude	
Terrain	
Cell Phone Reception / Carrier	

☐First Visit ☐Return Visit	Personal Rating	☐ Easy ☐Intermediat ☐Difficult

HIKING

Companion/s	
Facilities / Water Availability	
Trail & Weather Conditions	
Obesrvances	
Gear	
Food & Beverages	

Notes For Next Time

Notes / Journaling

HIKING

Date

Start Time	
End Time	
Total Duration	
Total Distance	
Elevation Gain/Loss	

Trail Type	Out/Back	Loop	One Way/ Shuttle

Weather	☐ Cold ☐ Hot ☐ Mild

The Hike ☆☆☆☆☆

City / State	
Trail/s	
Start Latitude Longitude	
Terrain	
Cell Phone Reception / Carrier	

☐First Visit ☐Return Visit | Personal Rating | ☐ Easy ☐Intermediat ☐Difficult

Companion/s	
Facilities / Water Availability	
Trail & Weather Conditions	
Obesrvances	
Gear	
Food & Beverages	

Notes For Next Time

Notes / Journaling

Date

Start Time	
End Time	
Total Duration	
Total Distance	
Elevation Gain/Loss	

Trail Type	Out/Back	Loop	One Way/ Shuttle

Weather ☐ Cold ☐ Hot ☐ Mild

The Hike ☆☆☆☆☆

City / State	
Trail/s	
Start Latitude Longitude	
Terrain	
Cell Phone Reception / Carrier	

☐First Visit ☐Return Visit | Personal Rating ☐ Easy ☐Intermediat☐Difficult

Companion/s	
Facilities / Water Availability	
Trail & Weather Conditions	
Obesrvances	
Gear	
Food & Beverages	

Notes For Next Time

Notes / Journaling

HIKING

Date

Start Time	
End Time	
Total Duration	
Total Distance	
Elevation Gain/Loss	

Trail Type	Out/Back	Loop	One Way/ Shuttle

Weather ☐ Cold ☐ Hot ☐ Mild

The Hike ☆☆☆☆☆

City / State	
Trail/s	
Start Latitude Longitude	
Terrain	
Cell Phone Reception / Carrier	

☐First Visit ☐Return Visit | **Personal Rating** | ☐ Easy ☐Intermediat ☐Difficult

Companion/s	
Facilities / Water Availability	
Trail & Weather Conditions	
Obesrvances	
Gear	
Food & Beverages	

Notes For Next Time

Notes / Journaling

Date

Start Time	
End Time	
Total Duration	
Total Distance	
Elevation Gain/Loss	

Trail Type	Out/Back	Loop	One Way/ Shuttle

Weather ☐ Cold ☐ Hot ☐ Mild

The Hike ☆☆☆☆☆

City / State	
Trail/s	
Start Latitude Longitude	
Terrain	
Cell Phone Reception / Carrier	

☐First Visit ☐Return Visit | Personal Rating | ☐ Easy ☐Intermediat☐Difficult

HIKING

Companion/s	
Facilities / Water Availability	
Trail & Weather Conditions	
Obesrvances	
Gear	
Food & Beverages	

Notes For Next Time

Notes / Journaling

HIKING

Date

Start Time	
End Time	
Total Duration	
Total Distance	
Elevation Gain/Loss	

Trail Type	Out/Back	Loop	One Way/ Shuttle

Weather   ☐ Cold ☐ Hot ☐ Mild

The Hike   ☆☆☆☆☆

City / State	
Trail/s	
Start Latitude Longitude	
Terrain	
Cell Phone Reception / Carrier	

☐First Visit ☐Return Visit | **Personal Rating** | ☐ Easy ☐Intermediat ☐Difficult

Companion/s	
Facilities / Water Availability	
Trail & Weather Conditions	
Obesrvances	
Gear	
Food & Beverages	

Notes For Next Time

Notes / Journaling

Date

Start Time	
End Time	
Total Duration	
Total Distance	
Elevation Gain/Loss	

Trail Type	Out/Back	Loop	One Way/ Shuttle

Weather ☐ Cold ☐ Hot ☐ Mild

The Hike ☆☆☆☆☆

City / State	
Trail/s	
Start Latitude Longitude	
Terrain	
Cell Phone Reception / Carrier	

☐First Visit ☐Return Visit | Personal Rating ☐ Easy ☐Intermediat ☐Difficult

HIKING

Companion/s	
Facilities / Water Availability	
Trail & Weather Conditions	
Obesrvances	
Gear	
Food & Beverages	

Notes For Next Time

Notes / Journaling

Date

Start Time			
End Time			
Total Duration			
Total Distance			
Elevation Gain/Loss			
Trail Type	Out/Back	Loop	One Way/ Shuttle

Weather   ☐ Cold ☐ Hot ☐ Mild

The Hike   ☆☆☆☆☆

City / State	
Trail/s	
Start Latitude Longitude	
Terrain	
Cell Phone Reception / Carrier	

☐First Visit ☐Return Visit | **Personal Rating** | ☐ Easy ☐Intermediat ☐Difficult

Companion/s	
Facilities / Water Availability	
Trail & Weather Conditions	
Obesrvances	
Gear	
Food & Beverages	

Notes For Next Time

Notes / Journaling

Date

Start Time	
End Time	
Total Duration	
Total Distance	
Elevation Gain/Loss	

Trail Type	Out/Back	Loop	One Way/ Shuttle

Weather ☐ Cold ☐ Hot ☐ Mild

The Hike ☆☆☆☆☆

City / State	
Trail/s	
Start Latitude Longitude	
Terrain	
Cell Phone Reception / Carrier	

☐First Visit ☐Return Visit | **Personal Rating** ☐ Easy ☐Intermediat☐Difficult

Companion/s	
Facilities / Water Availability	
Trail & Weather Conditions	
Obesrvances	
Gear	
Food & Beverages	

Notes For Next Time

Notes / Journaling

HIKING

Date

Start Time	
End Time	
Total Duration	
Total Distance	
Elevation Gain/Loss	

Trail Type	Out/Back	Loop	One Way/ Shuttle

Weather ☐ Cold ☐ Hot ☐ Mild

The Hike ☆☆☆☆☆

City / State	
Trail/s	
Start Latitude Longitude	
Terrain	
Cell Phone Reception / Carrier	

☐First Visit ☐Return Visit | **Personal Rating** | ☐ Easy ☐Intermediat ☐Difficult

Companion/s	
Facilities / Water Availability	
Trail & Weather Conditions	
Obesrvances	
Gear	
Food & Beverages	

Notes For Next Time

Notes / Journaling

HIKING

🏔	*Date*	🏔

Start Time			
End Time			
Total Duration			
Total Distance			
Elevation Gain/Loss			
Trail Type	Out/Back	Loop	One Way/ Shuttle

Weather ☐ Cold ☐ Hot ☐ Mild

🏔 *The Hike* ☆☆☆☆☆ 🏔

City / State	
Trail/s	
Start Latitude Longitude	
Terrain	
Cell Phone Reception / Carrier	

☐First Visit ☐Return Visit | **Personal Rating** ☐ Easy ☐Intermediat ☐Difficult

Companion/s	
Facilities / Water Availability	
Trail & Weather Conditions	
Obesrvances	
Gear	
Food & Beverages	

Notes For Next Time

Notes / Journaling

HIKING

Start Time	
End Time	
Total Duration	
Total Distance	
Elevation Gain/Loss	

Trail Type	Out/Back	Loop	One Way/ Shuttle

Weather   ☐ Cold   ☐ Hot   ☐ Mild

The Hike   ☆☆☆☆☆

City / State	
Trail/s	
Start Latitude Longitude	
Terrain	
Cell Phone Reception / Carrier	

☐First Visit ☐Return Visit **Personal Rating** ☐ Easy ☐Intermediat ☐Difficult

HIKING

Companion/s	
Facilities / Water Availability	
Trail & Weather Conditions	
Obesrvances	
Gear	
Food & Beverages	

Notes For Next Time

Notes / Journaling

HIKING

	Date

Start Time	
End Time	
Total Duration	
Total Distance	
Elevation Gain/Loss	

Trail Type	Out/Back	Loop	One Way/ Shuttle

Weather ☐ Cold ☐ Hot ☐ Mild

The Hike ☆☆☆☆☆

City / State	
Trail/s	
Start Latitude Longitude	
Terrain	
Cell Phone Reception / Carrier	

☐First Visit ☐Return Visit | Personal Rating | ☐ Easy ☐Intermediat☐Difficult

Companion/s	
Facilities / Water Availability	
Trail & Weather Conditions	
Obesrvances	
Gear	
Food & Beverages	

Notes For Next Time

Notes / Journaling

HIKING

Date	

Start Time	
End Time	
Total Duration	
Total Distance	
Elevation Gain/Loss	

Trail Type	Out/Back	Loop	One Way/ Shuttle

Weather ☐ Cold ☐ Hot ☐ Mild

The Hike ☆☆☆☆☆

City / State	
Trail/s	
Start Latitude Longitude	
Terrain	
Cell Phone Reception / Carrier	

☐First Visit ☐Return Visit **Personal Rating** ☐ Easy ☐Intermediat ☐Difficult

Companion/s	
Facilities / Water Availability	
Trail & Weather Conditions	
Obesrvances	
Gear	
Food & Beverages	

Notes For Next Time

Notes / Journaling

Date

Start Time	
End Time	
Total Duration	
Total Distance	
Elevation Gain/Loss	

Trail Type	Out/Back	Loop	One Way/ Shuttle

Weather ☐ Cold ☐ Hot ☐ Mild

The Hike ☆☆☆☆☆

City / State	
Trail/s	
Start Latitude Longitude	
Terrain	
Cell Phone Reception / Carrier	

☐First Visit ☐Return Visit | **Personal Rating** ☐ Easy ☐Intermediat☐Difficult

Companion/s	
Facilities / Water Availability	
Trail & Weather Conditions	
Obesrvances	
Gear	
Food & Beverages	

Notes For Next Time

Notes / Journaling

HIKING

Date	

Start Time	
End Time	
Total Duration	
Total Distance	
Elevation Gain/Loss	

Trail Type	Out/Back	Loop	One Way/ Shuttle

Weather ☐ Cold ☐ Hot ☐ Mild

The Hike ☆☆☆☆☆

City / State	
Trail/s	
Start Latitude Longitude	
Terrain	
Cell Phone Reception / Carrier	

☐First Visit ☐Return Visit | **Personal Rating** ☐ Easy ☐Intermediat ☐Difficult

Companion/s	
Facilities / Water Availability	
Trail & Weather Conditions	
Obesrvances	
Gear	
Food & Beverages	

Notes For Next Time

Notes / Journaling

Date

Start Time	
End Time	
Total Duration	
Total Distance	
Elevation Gain/Loss	

Trail Type	Out/Back	Loop	One Way/ Shuttle

Weather ☐ Cold ☐ Hot ☐ Mild

The Hike ☆☆☆☆☆☆

City / State	
Trail/s	
Start Latitude Longitude	
Terrain	
Cell Phone Reception / Carrier	

☐First Visit ☐Return Visit | Personal Rating ☐ Easy ☐Intermediat ☐Difficult

Companion/s	
Facilities / Water Availability	
Trail & Weather Conditions	
Obesrvances	
Gear	
Food & Beverages	

Notes For Next Time

Notes / Journaling

HIKING

Date

Start Time	
End Time	
Total Duration	
Total Distance	
Elevation Gain/Loss	

Trail Type	Out/Back	Loop	One Way/ Shuttle

Weather ☐ Cold ☐ Hot ☐ Mild

The Hike ☆☆☆☆☆

City / State	
Trail/s	
Start Latitude Longitude	
Terrain	
Cell Phone Reception / Carrier	

☐First Visit ☐Return Visit | **Personal Rating** | ☐ Easy ☐Intermediat ☐Difficult

Companion/s	
Facilities / Water Availability	
Trail & Weather Conditions	
Obesrvances	
Gear	
Food & Beverages	

Notes For Next Time

Notes / Journaling

HIKING

Date

Start Time	
End Time	
Total Duration	
Total Distance	
Elevation Gain/Loss	

Trail Type	Out/Back	Loop	One Way/ Shuttle

Weather ☐ Cold ☐ Hot ☐ Mild

The Hike ☆☆☆☆☆

City / State	
Trail/s	
Start Latitude Longitude	
Terrain	
Cell Phone Reception / Carrier	

☐First Visit ☐Return Visit | **Personal Rating** ☐ Easy ☐Intermediat☐Difficult

HIKING

Companion/s	
Facilities / Water Availability	
Trail & Weather Conditions	
Obesrvances	
Gear	
Food & Beverages	

Notes For Next Time

Notes / Journaling

HIKING

Date

Start Time	
End Time	
Total Duration	
Total Distance	
Elevation Gain/Loss	

Trail Type	Out/Back	Loop	One Way/ Shuttle

Weather ☐ Cold ☐ Hot ☐ Mild

The Hike ☆☆☆☆☆

City / State	
Trail/s	
Start Latitude Longitude	
Terrain	
Cell Phone Reception / Carrier	

☐First Visit ☐Return Visit | **Personal Rating** | ☐ Easy ☐Intermediat ☐Difficult

Companion/s	
Facilities / Water Availability	
Trail & Weather Conditions	
Obesrvances	
Gear	
Food & Beverages	

Notes For Next Time

Notes / Journaling

Date

Start Time	
End Time	
Total Duration	
Total Distance	
Elevation Gain/Loss	

Trail Type	Out/Back	Loop	One Way/ Shuttle

Weather   ☐ Cold ☐ Hot ☐ Mild

The Hike   ☆☆☆☆☆

City / State	
Trail/s	
Start Latitude Longitude	
Terrain	
Cell Phone Reception / Carrier	

☐First Visit ☐Return Visit | Personal Rating ☐ Easy ☐Intermediat ☐Difficult

Companion/s	
Facilities / Water Availability	
Trail & Weather Conditions	
Obesrvances	
Gear	
Food & Beverages	

Notes For Next Time

Notes / Journaling

HIKING

Date

Start Time	
End Time	
Total Duration	
Total Distance	
Elevation Gain/Loss	

Trail Type	Out/Back	Loop	One Way/ Shuttle

Weather ☐ Cold ☐ Hot ☐ Mild

The Hike ☆☆☆☆☆

City / State	
Trail/s	
Start Latitude Longitude	
Terrain	
Cell Phone Reception / Carrier	

☐First Visit ☐Return Visit | **Personal Rating** ☐ Easy ☐Intermediat ☐Difficult

Companion/s	
Facilities / Water Availability	
Trail & Weather Conditions	
Obesrvances	
Gear	
Food & Beverages	

Notes For Next Time

Notes / Journaling

HIKING

Date	

Start Time	
End Time	
Total Duration	
Total Distance	
Elevation Gain/Loss	

Trail Type	Out/Back	Loop	One Way/ Shuttle

Weather ☐ Cold ☐ Hot ☐ Mild

The Hike ☆☆☆☆☆

City / State	
Trail/s	
Start Latitude Longitude	
Terrain	
Cell Phone Reception / Carrier	

☐First Visit ☐Return Visit | **Personal Rating** ☐ Easy ☐Intermediat ☐Difficult

HIKING

Companion/s	
Facilities / Water Availability	
Trail & Weather Conditions	
Obesrvances	
Gear	
Food & Beverages	

Notes For Next Time

Notes / Journaling

HIKING

Date	

Start Time	
End Time	
Total Duration	
Total Distance	
Elevation Gain/Loss	

Trail Type	Out/Back	Loop	One Way/ Shuttle

Weather ☐ Cold ☐ Hot ☐ Mild

The Hike ☆☆☆☆☆

City / State	
Trail/s	
Start Latitude Longitude	
Terrain	
Cell Phone Reception / Carrier	

☐First Visit ☐Return Visit | **Personal Rating** | ☐ Easy ☐Intermediat ☐Difficult

Companion/s	
Facilities / Water Availability	
Trail & Weather Conditions	
Obesrvances	
Gear	
Food & Beverages	

Notes For Next Time

Notes / Journaling

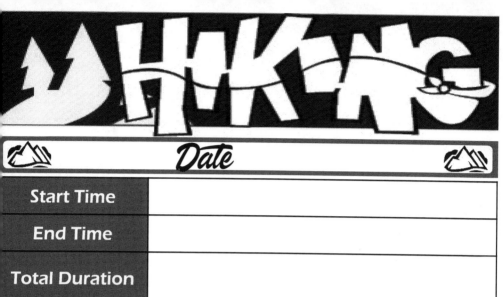

HIKING

	Date

Start Time	
End Time	
Total Duration	
Total Distance	
Elevation Gain/Loss	

Trail Type	Out/Back	Loop	One Way/ Shuttle

Weather ☐ Cold ☐ Hot ☐ Mild

The Hike ☆☆☆☆☆

City / State	
Trail/s	
Start Latitude Longitude	
Terrain	
Cell Phone Reception / Carrier	

☐First Visit ☐Return Visit | Personal Rating ☐ Easy ☐ Intermediat ☐ Difficult

Companion/s	
Facilities / Water Availability	
Trail & Weather Conditions	
Obesrvances	
Gear	
Food & Beverages	

Notes For Next Time

Notes / Journaling

HIKING

	Date	

Start Time	
End Time	
Total Duration	
Total Distance	
Elevation Gain/Loss	

	Out/Back	Loop	One Way/ Shuttle
Trail Type			

Weather ☐ Cold ☐ Hot ☐ Mild

The Hike ☆☆☆☆☆

City / State	
Trail/s	
Start Latitude Longitude	
Terrain	
Cell Phone Reception / Carrier	

☐ First Visit ☐ Return Visit | **Personal Rating** | ☐ Easy ☐ Intermediat ☐ Difficult

Companion/s	
Facilities / Water Availability	
Trail & Weather Conditions	
Obesrvances	
Gear	
Food & Beverages	

Notes For Next Time

Notes / Journaling

HIKING

Date	

Start Time	
End Time	
Total Duration	
Total Distance	
Elevation Gain/Loss	

Trail Type	Out/Back	Loop	One Way/ Shuttle

Weather ☐ Cold ☐ Hot ☐ Mild

The Hike ☆☆☆☆☆

City / State	
Trail/s	
Start Latitude Longitude	
Terrain	
Cell Phone Reception / Carrier	

☐First Visit ☐Return Visit | **Personal Rating** ☐ Easy ☐Intermediat ☐Difficult

Companion/s	
Facilities / Water Availability	
Trail & Weather Conditions	
Obesrvances	
Gear	
Food & Beverages	

Notes For Next Time

Notes / Journaling

HIKING

	Date

Start Time	
End Time	
Total Duration	
Total Distance	
Elevation Gain/Loss	

Trail Type	Out/Back	Loop	One Way/ Shuttle

Weather	☐ Cold ☐ Hot ☐ Mild

The Hike   ☆☆☆☆☆

City / State	
Trail/s	
Start Latitude Longitude	
Terrain	
Cell Phone Reception / Carrier	

☐First Visit ☐Return Visit	**Personal Rating**	☐ Easy ☐Intermediat ☐Difficult

Companion/s	
Facilities / Water Availability	
Trail & Weather Conditions	
Obesrvances	
Gear	
Food & Beverages	

Notes For Next Time

Notes / Journaling

HIKING

	Date

Start Time	
End Time	
Total Duration	
Total Distance	
Elevation Gain/Loss	

Trail Type	Out/Back	Loop	One Way/ Shuttle

Weather ☐ Cold ☐ Hot ☐ Mild

The Hike ☆☆☆☆☆

City / State	
Trail/s	
Start Latitude Longitude	
Terrain	
Cell Phone Reception / Carrier	

☐First Visit ☐Return Visit | **Personal Rating** ☐ Easy ☐Intermediat☐Difficult

Companion/s	
Facilities / Water Availability	
Trail & Weather Conditions	
Obesrvances	
Gear	
Food & Beverages	

Notes For Next Time

Notes / Journaling

HIKING

Date	

Start Time			
End Time			
Total Duration			
Total Distance			
Elevation Gain/Loss			
Trail Type	Out/Back	Loop	One Way/ Shuttle

Weather ☐ Cold ☐ Hot ☐ Mild

The Hike ☆☆☆☆☆

City / State	
Trail/s	
Start Latitude Longitude	
Terrain	
Cell Phone Reception / Carrier	

☐First Visit ☐Return Visit | **Personal Rating** ☐ Easy ☐Intermediat ☐Difficult

Companion/s	
Facilities / Water Availability	
Trail & Weather Conditions	
Obesrvances	
Gear	
Food & Beverages	

Notes For Next Time

Notes / Journaling

_____
_____
_____
_____
_____
_____
_____
_____
_____
_____
_____
_____
_____
_____
_____
_____
_____
_____
_____
_____
_____
_____
_____
_____
_____
_____
_____
_____
_____
_____

HIKING

Date

Start Time	
End Time	
Total Duration	
Total Distance	
Elevation Gain/Loss	

Trail Type	Out/Back	Loop	One Way/ Shuttle

Weather ☐ Cold ☐ Hot ☐ Mild

The Hike ☆☆☆☆☆

City / State	
Trail/s	
Start Latitude Longitude	
Terrain	
Cell Phone Reception / Carrier	

☐First Visit ☐Return Visit	**Personal Rating**	☐ Easy ☐Intermediat ☐Difficult

Companion/s	
Facilities / Water Availability	
Trail & Weather Conditions	
Obesrvances	
Gear	
Food & Beverages	

Notes For Next Time

Notes / Journaling

HIKING

Start Time	
End Time	
Total Duration	
Total Distance	
Elevation Gain/Loss	

Trail Type	Out/Back	Loop	One Way/ Shuttle

Weather ☐ Cold ☐ Hot ☐ Mild

The Hike ☆☆☆☆☆

City / State	
Trail/s	
Start Latitude Longitude	
Terrain	
Cell Phone Reception / Carrier	

☐First Visit ☐Return Visit | **Personal Rating** | ☐ Easy ☐Intermediat ☐Difficult

Companion/s	
Facilities / Water Availability	
Trail & Weather Conditions	
Obesrvances	
Gear	
Food & Beverages	

Notes For Next Time

Notes / Journaling

_____
_____
_____
_____
_____
_____
_____
_____
_____
_____
_____
_____
_____
_____
_____
_____
_____
_____
_____
_____
_____
_____
_____
_____
_____
_____
_____
_____
_____
_____
_____
_____

HIKING

Start Time	
End Time	
Total Duration	
Total Distance	
Elevation Gain/Loss	

Trail Type	Out/Back	Loop	One Way/ Shuttle

Weather

☐ Cold ☐ Hot ☐ Mild

The Hike ☆☆☆☆☆

City / State	
Trail/s	
Start Latitude Longitude	
Terrain	
Cell Phone Reception / Carrier	

☐First Visit ☐Return Visit	Personal Rating ☐ Easy ☐Intermediat ☐Difficult

HIKING

Companion/s	
Facilities / Water Availability	
Trail & Weather Conditions	
Obesrvances	
Gear	
Food & Beverages	

Notes For Next Time

Notes / Journaling

HIKING

Date	

Start Time	
End Time	
Total Duration	
Total Distance	
Elevation Gain/Loss	

Trail Type	Out/Back	Loop	One Way/ Shuttle

Weather	☐ Cold ☐ Hot ☐ Mild

The Hike ☆☆☆☆☆

City / State	
Trail/s	
Start Latitude Longitude	
Terrain	
Cell Phone Reception / Carrier	

☐First Visit ☐Return Visit	**Personal Rating**	☐ Easy ☐Intermediat ☐Difficult

Companion/s	
Facilities / Water Availability	
Trail & Weather Conditions	
Obesrvances	
Gear	
Food & Beverages	

Notes For Next Time

Notes / Journaling

Date

Start Time			
End Time			
Total Duration			
Total Distance			
Elevation Gain/Loss			
Trail Type	Out/Back	Loop	One Way/ Shuttle

Weather ☐ Cold ☐ Hot ☐ Mild

The Hike ☆☆☆☆☆

City / State	
Trail/s	
Start Latitude Longitude	
Terrain	
Cell Phone Reception / Carrier	

☐First Visit ☐Return Visit | **Personal Rating** ☐ Easy ☐Intermediat☐Difficult

Companion/s	
Facilities / Water Availability	
Trail & Weather Conditions	
Obesrvances	
Gear	
Food & Beverages	

Notes For Next Time

Notes / Journaling

HIKING

Start Time	
End Time	
Total Duration	
Total Distance	
Elevation Gain/Loss	

Trail Type	Out/Back	Loop	One Way/ Shuttle

Weather ☐ Cold ☐ Hot ☐ Mild

The Hike ☆☆☆☆☆

City / State	
Trail/s	
Start Latitude Longitude	
Terrain	
Cell Phone Reception / Carrier	

☐First Visit ☐Return Visit | **Personal Rating** ☐ Easy ☐Intermediat ☐Difficult

HIKING

Companion/s	
Facilities / Water Availability	
Trail & Weather Conditions	
Obesrvances	
Gear	
Food & Beverages	

Notes For Next Time

Notes / Journaling

HIKING

Date

Start Time	
End Time	
Total Duration	
Total Distance	
Elevation Gain/Loss	

Trail Type	Out/Back	Loop	One Way/ Shuttle

Weather ☐ Cold ☐ Hot ☐ Mild

The Hike ☆☆☆☆☆

City / State	
Trail/s	
Start Latitude Longitude	
Terrain	
Cell Phone Reception / Carrier	

☐First Visit ☐Return Visit | **Personal Rating** | ☐ Easy ☐Intermediat ☐Difficult

Companion/s	
Facilities / Water Availability	
Trail & Weather Conditions	
Obesrvances	
Gear	
Food & Beverages	

Notes For Next Time

Notes / Journaling